CREATION'S KALEIDOSCOPE

Embracing Light Verse Journal

Deborah A. Goshorn-Stenger

Our mission is to share the love of Jesus through His Word, nature, and creativity. We believe that God's beauty is all around us if we'll pause to see it and give Him honor and praise.

2 Pause and Praise Creations

Your Free Book is Waiting!

Are you seeking to develop a more intimate Prayer Life with Jesus? Do you want to know what God's Word says about Prayer? Then this beautifully illustrated book is for you!

This "Pray-it-Through" Verse style of Devotional combines a Word Search Puzzle, Sketch Art, and full-size Coloring Pages to create an innovative way *2 Pause and Praise* the Lord. This 72-page offering is a prequel for Deb's other full-size Word Search Puzzle Books. *On Wings of Prayer* will deepen your conversations with the Lord. Here, you'll be encouraged to get into God's Word and sink His precious truths into your heart!

Get your free copy of *On Wings of Prayer* here:

Preface

We had just completed the *Creation's Kaleidoscope: Embracing Light Devotional* and its companion *Journal.* Doug and I were reflecting on the lovely promises from Scripture. We thought about all the various scenes and pictures that had become so special to us. Together, we had the idea to create a double-sided open-style Verse Journal.

What if we could use God's Word and His lovely creations to record our prayer requests and how He answers us? What if we use the idea (from the *Creation's Kaleidoscope Devotionals* and full *Journals*) to explore how to write "Thank You's" to the Lord daily? How about taking this little volume along so you can journal at work or in the park? Ideas were swiftly filling my mind.

Precious Scriptures accompany each watercolor-like scene. This Verse Journal gives you the perfect way to draw into the company of God. See and record His faithfulness and the insights from His Spirit and Word!

Turn the page to the "How to use Guide" for more ideas.

Think of these pages as a place to "pause and praise" each day ... to reflect and to express gratitude for God's faithfulness, grace, mercy, and love. *"The loyal love of Yahweh does not cease; his compassions do not come to an end. They are new in the morning, great is your faithfulness" (Lamentations 3:23-24 LEB).*

List your prayer requests and "talk your heart to God" over each one. Remember to make notes as He answers! *"Pray continually, give thanks in all circumstances; for this is God's will for you in Christ Jesus" (1 Thessalonians 5:17-18 NIV).*

Remember to pray for your friends, family, neighbors, co-workers, classmates, missionaries, our nation, and for God to use you to be His instrument of joy, healing, love, and peace today. *"I thank my God for you every time I think of you" (Philippians 1:3).*

Write a "Thank You" note to the Lord as a method for journaling the ways He is blessing your life daily. Want a simple way to get started? How about noticing at least three things, people, or circumstances where you see God's presence? *"Every good thing given and every perfect gift is from above; it comes down from the Father of lights [the Creator and Sustainer of the heavens], in whom there is no variation [no rising or setting] or shadow cast by His turning [for He is perfect and never changes]" (James 1:17 AMP).*

Use the front to guide your errands or grocery list ... then on the reverse, when you return home ... list a few ways God provided for your emotional and spiritual needs while you were out. *"And my God will supply all your needs according to His riches in glory in Christ Jesus" (Philippians 4:19 NASB).*

Take the *Creation's Kaleidoscope* Verse Journal along at lunchtime or on a break (to a park or your backyard) to meditate and journal on the provided Verses or creation. Explore how the Lord is speaking His truths into your life. *"Let the words of my mouth and the meditation of my heart be acceptable in Your sight, O Lord, my strength and my Redeemer" (Psalm 19:14 NKJV).*

Use these pages to write out God's promises that you are working on memorizing. Tape them on your mirror or tuck them in a pocket, and fill your mind with His love and light. *"Imprint these words of mine on your hearts and minds, bind them as a sign on your hands, and let them be a symbol on your foreheads" (Deuteronomy 11:18 HCSB).*

May every line you write remind you that God's love surrounds you—to bring you the facets of His love.

A Verse Journal Meditation

Dear Lord, as I use these journaling pages, help me pause and appreciate the nearness of Your presence. Please help me notice how You are providing for me. Teach me to see the time that I invest here as a way to grow in my faith. Work in my heart, Jesus. As I meditate upon Your Word, talk to You, and journal —I'm committing to spend time in Your company. As I count Your gracious blessings, I will be creating a written record of how You are answering my prayers and how faithful You are every day. Let this Journal—bring You honor and praise—I pray. Amen.

Copyright

Creation's Kaleidoscope: Embracing Light Verse Journal (Volume I): ISBN: 978-1-954690-02-8

Requests for information should be directed to:
2 Pause and Praise Creations
5315 Long Street, Suite 518
McFarland, WI 53558

Also by *Deborah Goshorn-Stenger*

The *Creation's Kaleidoscope* Series

The Devotional Word Search Puzzle Book Collection

The Purry Companion Series

You can find all the details on books in these series, and more at:
www.2PauseandPraiseCreations.com/books

or simply point your phone camera at the QR code (below), which will take you directly to our Website Books page

To Contact us: 2PauseandPraiseCreations.com
or by mail at:
2 Pause and Praise Creations
5315 Long St, Suite 518
McFarland, WI 53558

"The Lord bless you and keep you; the Lord make His face shine upon you, and be gracious to you; the Lord lift up His countenance upon you, and give you peace." Numbers 6:24-26 NKJV

....
....
....
....
....
....
....
....
....
....
....
....
....
....
....
....
....
....
....
....
....

*"Let the morning bring me word of your unfailing love,
for I have put my trust in you. Show me the way I should
go, for to you I entrust my life." Psalm 143:8 (NIV)*

....

....

....

....

....

....

....

....

....

....

....

....

....

....

....

....

....

....

....

....

....

....

....

"For behold, He who forms mountains and creates the wind and declares to man what are His thoughts, He who makes dawn into darkness and treads on the high places of the earth, the Lord God of hosts is His name." Amos 4:13 (NASB)

....

....

....

....

....

....

....

....

....

....

....

....

....

....

....

....

....

....

....

"For this reason we have not stopped praying for you since the day we heard about you. We ask God to fill you with the knowledge of his will through every kind of spiritual wisdom and insight. We ask this so that you will live the kind of lives that prove you belong to the Lord. Then you will want to please him in every way as you grow in producing every kind of good work by this knowledge about God." Colossians 1:9-10 (GW)

....

....

....

....

....

....

....

....

....

....

....

....

....

....

....

....

....

....

....

....

....

....

....

....

"But you are a chosen people, a royal priesthood, a holy nation, God's special possession, that you may declare the praises of him who called you out of darkness into his wonderful light." 1 Peter 2:9 (NIV)

....
....
....
....
....
....
....
....
....
....
....
....
....
....
....
....
....
....
....
....
....
....

"A light shines in the dark for honest people. It shines for those who are good and kind and merciful." Psalm 112:4 (ICB)

....
....
....
....
....
....
....
....
....
....
....
....
....
....
....
....
....
....
....
....
....
....

"For once you were darkness, but now you are light in the Lord; walk as children of Light [live as those who are native-born to the Light] (for the fruit [the effect, the result] of the Light consists in all goodness and righteousness and truth) …" Ephesians 5:8-9 (AMP)

....
....
....
....
....
....
....
....
....
....
....
....
....
....
....
....
....
....
....
....
....

"Satisfy us in the morning with your steadfast love, that we may rejoice and be glad all our days." Psalm 90:14 (ESV)

....

....

....

....

....

....

....

....

....

....

....

....

....

....

....

....

....

....

....

....

....

"He assigned the moon to mark the months and
the sun to mark the days." Psalm 104:19 (TLB)

....
....
....
....
....
....
....
....
....
....
....
....
....
....
....
....
....
....
....
....
....

"From the rising of the sun to its setting, the name of the Lord is to be praised." Psalm 113:3 (NASB)

....

....

....

....

....

....

....

....

....

....

....

....

....

....

....

....

....

....

....

....

....

"When Jesus spoke again to the people, he said, 'I am the light of the world. Whoever follows me will never walk in darkness, but will have the light of life.'" John 8:12 (NIV)

....
....
....
....
....
....
....
....
....
....
....
....
....
....
....
....
....
....
....
....
....
....
....
....

"When he sneezes, the sunlight sparkles like lightning across the vapor droplets. His eyes glow like sparks." Job 41:18 (TLB)

....
....
....
....
....
....
....
....
....
....
....
....
....
....
....
....
....
....
....
....
....
....

"Commit your way to the Lord, trust also in Him, and He shall bring it to pass. He shall bring forth your righteousness as the light, and your justice as the noonday." Psalm 37:5-6 (NJKV)

··

··

··

··

··

··

··

··

··

··

··

··

··

··

··

··

··

··

··

"Then, oh then, your light will break out like the warm, golden rays of a rising sun; in an instant, you will be healed. Your rightness will precede and protect you; the glory of the Eternal will follow and defend

....

....

....

....

....

....

....

....

....

....

....

....

....

....

....

....

....

....

....

....

....

....

....

....

"There he was transfigured before them. His face shone like the sun, and his clothes became as white as the light." Matthew 17:2 (NIV)

....
....
....
....
....
....
....
....
....
....
....
....
....
....
....
....
....
....
....
....
....
....

"The Lord provides the sun for light by day, the moon and the stars to shine at night. He stirs up the sea and makes it roar; his name is the Lord Almighty." Jeremiah 31:35 (GNT)

....
....
....
....
....
....
....
....
....
....
....
....
....
....
....
....
....
....
....
....
....
....

"The people walking in darkness have seen a great light; a light has dawned on those living in the land of darkness." Isaiah 9:2 (HCSB)

....
....
....
....
....
....
....
....
....
....
....
....
....
....
....
....
....
....
....
....
....

"All this will be because the mercy of our God is very tender, and heaven's dawn is about to break upon us, to give light to those who sit in darkness and death's shadow, and to guide us to the path of peace." Luke 1:78-79 (TLB)

....
....
....
....
....
....
....
....
....
....
....
....
....
....
....
....
....
....
....
....
....
....
....
....

"But as for me, I will sing of your strength, and I will hail your loyal love in the morning, because you have been my high stronghold and a refuge in my time of trouble." Psalm 59:16 (LEB)

....
....
....
....
....
....
....
....
....
....
....
....
....
....
....
....
....
....
....
....

"The Word was the source of life, and this life brought light to people. The light shines in the darkness, and the darkness has never put it out." John 1:4-5 (GNT)

....
....
....
....
....
....
....
....
....
....
....
....
....
....
....
....
....
....
....
....
....
....

"… I will guide them in paths that they do not know. I will make darkness into light before them and rugged places into plains. These things I will do [for them], and I will not leave them abandoned or undone." Isaiah 42:16 (AMP)

....
....
....
....
....
....
....
....
....
....
....
....
....
....
....
....
....
....
....
....

"And God said, 'Let there be light,' and there was light. God saw that the light was good, and he separated the light from the darkness. God called the light 'day,' and the darkness he called 'night.' And there was evening, and there was morning—the first day." Genesis 1:3-5 (NIV)

....
....
....
....
....
....
....
....
....
....
....
....
....
....
....
....
....
....
....
....
....
....
....

"Night is almost over, and day will soon appear. We must stop behaving as people do in the dark and be ready to live in the light." Romans 13:12 (CEV)

....
....
....
....
....
....
....
....
....
....
....
....
....
....
....
....
....
....
....
....
....
....
....
....
....
....

*"Whatever you have said in the dark will be heard in the light,
and what you have whispered behind closed doors will be
shouted from the housetops for all to hear!" Luke 12:3 (NLT)*

....

....

....

....

....

....

....

....

....

....

....

....

....

....

....

....

....

....

....

....

....

....

"This is the day the Lord has made. We will
rejoice and be glad in it." Psalm 118:24 (NLT)

....
....
....
....
....
....
....
....
....
....
....
....
....
....
....
....
....
....
....
....
....
....
....

*"Light shines on those who do right. Joy belongs
to those who are honest." Psalm 97:11 (ICB)*

....

....

....

....

....

....

....

....

....

....

....

....

....

....

....

....

....

....

....

....

....

....

"For this is what the Lord says, the one who created the sky—he is the true God, the one who formed the earth and made it; he established it, he did not create it without order, he formed it to be inhabited: 'I am the Lord, I have no peer.'" Isaiah 45:18 (NET)

....
....
....
....
....
....
....
....
....
....
....
....
....
....
....
....
....
....
....
....
....
....
....

"The Almighty God, the Lord, speaks; he calls to the whole earth from east to west." Psalm 50:1 (GNT)

....

....

....

....

....

....

....

....

....

....

....

....

....

....

....

....

....

....

"Make a joyful shout to the Lord, all you lands! Serve the Lord with gladness; come before His presence with singing. Know that the Lord, He is God; it is He who has made us, and not we ourselves; we are His people and the sheep of His pasture." Psalm 100:1-3 (NKJV)

....

....

....

....

....

....

....

....

....

....

....

....

....

....

....

....

....

....

....

....

....

....

*"I will lift up my eyes to the mountains; from where shall my help come?
My help comes from the Lord, Who made heaven and earth. He will not allow
your foot to slip; He who keeps you will not slumber." Psalm 121:1-3 (NASB)*

....

....

....

....

....

....

....

....

....

....

....

....

....

....

....

....

....

....

....

....

....

....

"There is a time for everything, and a season for every activity under the heavens: ... He has made everything beautiful in its time. He has also set eternity in the human heart; yet no one can fathom what God has done from beginning to end." Ecclesiastes 3:1, 11 (NIV)

....
....
....
....
....
....
....
....
....
....
....
....
....
....
....
....
....
....
....
....
....
....
....

"Praise the Lord, O heavens! Praise him from the skies! Praise him, all his angels, all the armies of heaven. Praise him, sun and moon and all you twinkling stars." Psalm 148:1-3 (TLB)

....

....

....

....

....

....

....

....

....

....

....

....

....

....

....

....

....

....

....

....

"Your lovingkindness and graciousness, O Lord, extend to the skies,
Your faithfulness [reaches] to the clouds." Psalm 36:5 (AMP)

....

....

....

....

....

....

....

....

....

....

....

....

....

....

....

....

....

....

....

....

....

*"God called the canopy 'sky.' The twilight and the
dawn were the second day." Genesis 1:8 (ISV)*

....
....
....
....
....
....
....
....
....
....
....
....
....
....
....
....
....
....
....
....

"You are as majestic as the morning sky—glorious as the moon—blinding as the sun! Your charms are more powerful than all the stars above." Song of Songs 6:10 (CEV)

....

....

....

....

....

....

....

....

....

....

....

....

....

....

....

....

....

....

....

....

....

....

....

"You are the Eternal, the only One. The skies are Your work alone—You made the heavens above those skies and the stars that fill them. You made the earth and everything upon it, the seas and all that lives within their depths. Your creation lives and is sustained by You, and those who dwell in the heavens, fall down before You and worship." Nehemiah 9:6 (VOICE)

....

....

....

....

....

....

....

....

....

....

....

....

....

....

....

....

....

....

....

....

....

"Your constant love reaches above the heavens; your faithfulness touches the skies." Psalm 108:4 (GNT)

....

....

....

....

....

....

....

....

....

....

....

....

....

....

....

....

....

....

....

"I look up at your macro-skies, dark and enormous, your handmade sky-jewelry, moon and stars mounted in their settings. Then I look at my micro-self and wonder, why do you bother with us? Why take a second look our way? Yet we've so narrowly missed being gods, bright with Eden's dawn light. You put us in charge of your handcrafted world, repeated to us your Genesis-charge, made us lords of sheep and cattle, even animals out in the wild, birds flying and fish swimming, whales singing in the ocean deeps." Psalm 8:3-8 (MSG)

....

....

....

....

....

....

....

....

....

....

....

....

....

....

....

....

....

....

....

....

....

....

....

*"He who made the Pleiades and Orion and changes deep darkness to morning.
Who darkens the day into night. Who summons the water of the sea and pours
it out on the face of the earth—Adonai is His Name." Amos 5:8 (TLV)*

....
....
....
....
....
....
....
....
....
....
....
....
....
....
....
....
....
....
....
....
....
....
....
....

"I have come as a light into the world, in order that everyone who believes in me will not remain in the darkness." John 12:46 (LEB)

....
....
....
....
....
....
....
....
....
....
....
....
....
....
....
....
....
....
....
....
....
....
....
....

"Every day I will bless You and lovingly praise You; yes, [with awe-inspired reverence] I will praise Your name forever and ever." Psalm 145:2 (AMP)

....
....
....
....
....
....
....
....
....
....
....
....
....
....
....
....
....
....
....
....
....
....
....
....

"[May the people fear You] for as long as the sun shines, as long as the moon rises in the night sky, throughout the generations." Psalm 72:5 (VOICE)

....
....
....
....
....
....
....
....
....
....
....
....
....
....
....
....
....
....
....
....
....

"Those who are wise will shine like the brightness of the heavens, and those who lead many to righteousness, like the stars for ever and ever." Daniel 12:3 (NIV)

....
....
....
....
....
....
....
....
....
....
....
....
....
....
....
....
....
....
....
....
....
....
....
....

"He counts the number of the stars; he gives names to all of them. Great is our Lord, and abundant in power; his understanding is unlimited." Psalm 147:4-5 (LEB)

....

....

....

....

....

....

....

....

....

....

....

....

....

....

....

....

....

....

"… Behold, the star, which they had seen in the east, went on before them [continually leading the way] until it came and stood over the place where the young Child was. When they saw the star, they rejoiced exceedingly with great joy. And after entering the house, they saw the Child with Mary His mother; and they fell down and worshiped Him. Then, after opening their treasure chests, they presented to Him gifts [fit for a king, gifts] of gold, frankincense, and myrrh." Matthew 2:9b-11 (AMP)

....
....
....
....
....
....
....
....
....
....
....
....
....
....
....
....
....
....
....
....
....
....

*"Create in me a clean heart, O God, and renew a
steadfast spirit within me."* Psalm 51:10 (NKJV)

....
....
....
....
....
....
....
....
....
....
....
....
....
....
....
....
....
....
....
....
....
....
....
....
....

"If we confess our sins, he is faithful and just and will forgive us our sins and purify us from all unrighteousness." 1 John 1:9 (NIV)

....
....
....
....
....
....
....
....
....
....
....
....
....
....
....
....
....
....
....
....
....
....
....
....

"The sky was made at the Lord's command. By the breath from his mouth, he made all the stars." Psalm 33:6 (ICB)

....
....
....
....
....
....
....
....
....
....
....
....
....
....
....
....
....
....

*"I will ask the Father to give you another Helper, to be with you
always. He is the Spirit of truth, whom the world cannot receive,
because it neither sees him nor recognizes him. But you recognize him,
because he lives with you and will be in you." John 14:16-17 (ISV)*

....

....

....

....

....

....

....

....

....

....

....

....

....

....

....

....

....

....

....

....

*"The heavens are telling of the glory of God; and their expanse
is declaring the work of His hands." Psalm 19:1 (NASB)*

"Therefore we do not lose heart. Even though our outward man is perishing, yet the inward man is being renewed day by day." 2 Corinthians 4:16 (NKJV)

....

....

....

....

....

....

....

....

....

....

....

....

....

....

....

....

....

....

....

....

....

....

....

"For nothing is concealed except to be revealed, and nothing hidden except to come to light." Mark 4:22 (HCSB)

....
....
....
....
....
....
....
....
....
....
....
....
....
....
....
....
....
....
....
....
....
....
....

"Your word is a lamp to my feet and a light to my path." Psalm 119:105 (ESV)

....
....
....
....
....
....
....
....
....
....
....
....
....
....
....
....
....
....
....
....
....

"And we all, with unveiled face, beholding the glory of the Lord, are being transformed into the same image from one degree of glory to another. For this comes from the Lord who is the Spirit." 2 Corinthians 3:18 (ESV)

....
....
....
....
....
....
....
....
....
....
....
....
....
....
....
....
....
....
....
....
....
....

"So here's what I want you to do, God helping you: Take your everyday, ordinary life—your sleeping, eating, going-to-work, and walking-around life—and place it before God as an offering. Embracing what God does for you is the best thing you can do for him." Romans 12:1-2 (MSG)

....

....

....

....

....

....

....

....

....

....

....

....

....

....

....

....

....

....

"It's who you are and the way you live that count before God. Your worship must engage your spirit in the pursuit of truth. That's the kind of people the Father is out looking for: those who are simply and honestly themselves before him in their worship. God is sheer being itself —Spirit. Those who worship him must do it out of their very being, their spirits, their true selves, in adoration." John 4:23-24 (MSG)

....
....
....
....
....
....
....
....
....
....
....
....
....
....
....
....
....
....
....
....
....
....
....

"For everything God created is good, and nothing is to be rejected if it is received with thanksgiving ..." 1 Timothy 4:4 (NIV)

....

....

....

....

....

....

....

....

....

....

....

....

....

....

....

....

....

....

....

*"May the Lord guide your hearts into God's pure love
and keep you headed straight into the strong and sure
grip of the Anointed One." 2 Thessalonians 3:5 (VOICE)*

....
....
....
....
....
....
....
....
....
....
....
....
....
....
....
....
....
....
....
....
....
....

*"And now these three remain: faith, hope and love. But the
greatest of these is love." 1 Corinthians 13:13 (NIV)*

....
....
....
....
....
....
....
....
....
....
....
....
....
....
....
....
....
....
....
....
....
....
....

*"Do not let kindness and truth leave you; bind them around your neck,
write them on the tablet of your heart. So you will find favor
and good repute in the sight of God and man." Proverbs 3:3-4 (NASB)*

....

....

....

....

....

....

....

....

....

....

....

....

....

....

....

....

....

....

....

....

"I pray that from his glorious, unlimited resources he will empower you with inner strength through his Spirit. Then Christ will make his home in your hearts as you trust in him. Your roots will grow down into God's love and keep you strong. And may you have the power to understand, as all God's people should, how wide, how long, how high, and how deep his love is." Ephesians 3:16-18 (NLT)

....
....
....
....
....
....
....
....
....
....
....
....
....
....
....
....
....
....
....
....
....
....
....
....
....

*"Cause me to hear Your lovingkindness in the morning, for in
You do I trust; cause me to know the way in which I should
walk, for I lift up my soul to You." Psalm 143:8 (NKJV)*

....

....

....

....

....

....

....

....

....

....

....

....

....

....

....

....

....

....

....

....

....

"Because your loyal love is better than life, my lips will praise you. So I will bless you while I live. I will lift up my hands in your name." Psalm 63:3-4 (LEB)

....
....
....
....
....
....
....
....
....
....
....
....
....
....
....
....
....
....
....
....
....

"Anyone who believes in me may come and drink! For the Scriptures declare, 'Rivers of living water will flow from his heart.'" John 7:38 (NLT)

....
....
....
....
....
....
....
....
....
....
....
....
....
....
....
....
....
....
....
....
....
....
....

"And above all these put on love, which binds everything together in perfect harmony." Colossians 3:14 (ESV)

....

....

....

....

....

....

....

....

....

....

....

....

....

....

....

....

....

....

....

....

"But you, dear friends, carefully build yourselves up in this most holy faith by praying in the Holy Spirit, staying right at the center of God's love, keeping your arms open and outstretched, ready for the mercy of our Master, Jesus Christ. This is the unending life, the real life!" Jude 1:20-21 (MSG)

....

....

....

....

....

....

....

....

....

....

....

....

....

....

....

....

....

....

....

....

....

....

....

*"The Lord your God in your midst, the Mighty One, will save; He
will rejoice over you with gladness, He will quiet you with His love,
He will rejoice over you with singing." Zephaniah 3:17 (NKJV)*

....

....

....

....

....

....

....

....

....

....

....

....

....

....

....

....

....

....

....

....

....

....

"Oh give thanks to Yahweh, for he is good; his loyal love is everlasting." 1 Chronicles 16:34 (LEB)

....

....

....

....

....

....

....

....

....

....

....

....

....

....

....

....

....

....

....

"For I am sure that neither death nor life, nor angels nor rulers, nor things present nor things to come, nor powers, nor height nor depth, nor anything else in all creation, will be able to separate us from the love of God in Christ Jesus our Lord." Romans 8:38-39 (ESV)

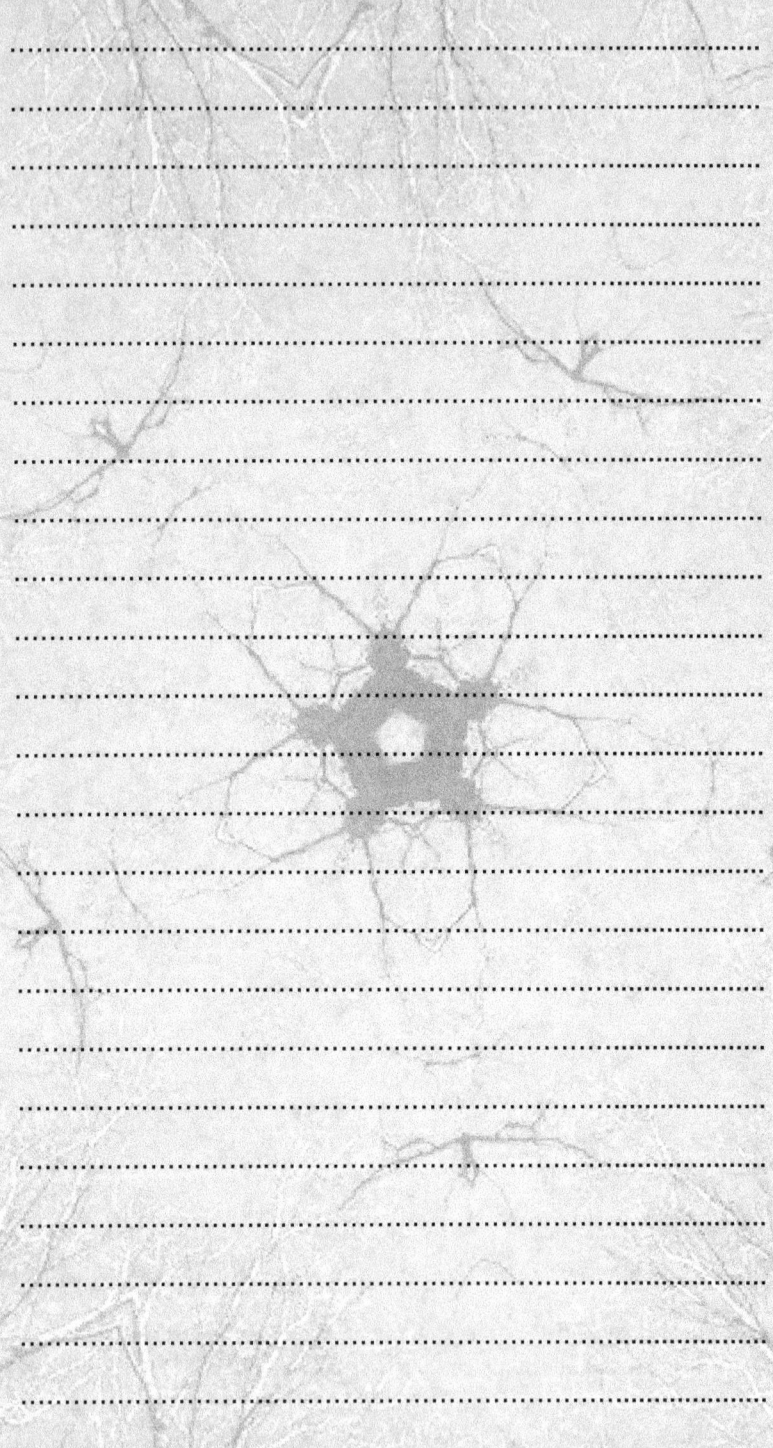

....
....
....
....
....
....
....
....
....
....
....
....
....
....
....
....
....
....
....
....

"Your steadfast love, O Lord, is as great as all the heavens. Your faithfulness reaches beyond the clouds. Your justice is as solid as God's mountains. Your decisions are as full of wisdom as the oceans are with water. You are concerned for men and animals alike." Psalm 36:5-6 (TLB)

....
....
....
....
....
....
....
....
....
....
....
....
....
....
....
....
....
....
....
....
....
....
....

"Give thanks to the Lord, because he is good,
and his love is eternal." Psalm 118:1 (GNT)

....

....

....

....

....

....

....

....

....

....

....

....

....

....

....

....

....

....

....

....

*"And you shall love the Lord your God with all your heart, and
with all your soul (life), and with all your mind (thought,
understanding), and with all your strength. This is the second:
'You shall [unselfishly] love your neighbor as yourself.' There is no
other commandment greater than these." Mark 12:30-31 (AMP)*

....

....

....

....

....

....

....

....

....

....

....

....

....

....

....

....

....

....

....

....

....

....

*"But as Scripture says: 'No eye has seen, no ear has heard,
and no mind has imagined the things that God has
prepared for those who love him.'" 1 Corinthians 2:9 (GW)*

....
....
....
....
....
....
....
....
....
....
....
....
....
....
....
....
....
....
....
....
....
....

"Show your kindness to me, your servant. Save me because of your love." Psalm 31:16 (ICB)

....

....

....

....

....

....

....

....

....

....

....

....

....

....

....

....

....

....

....

....

....

....

....

....

"Let everything you do be done in love [motivated and inspired by God's love for us]." 1 Corinthians 16:14 (AMP)

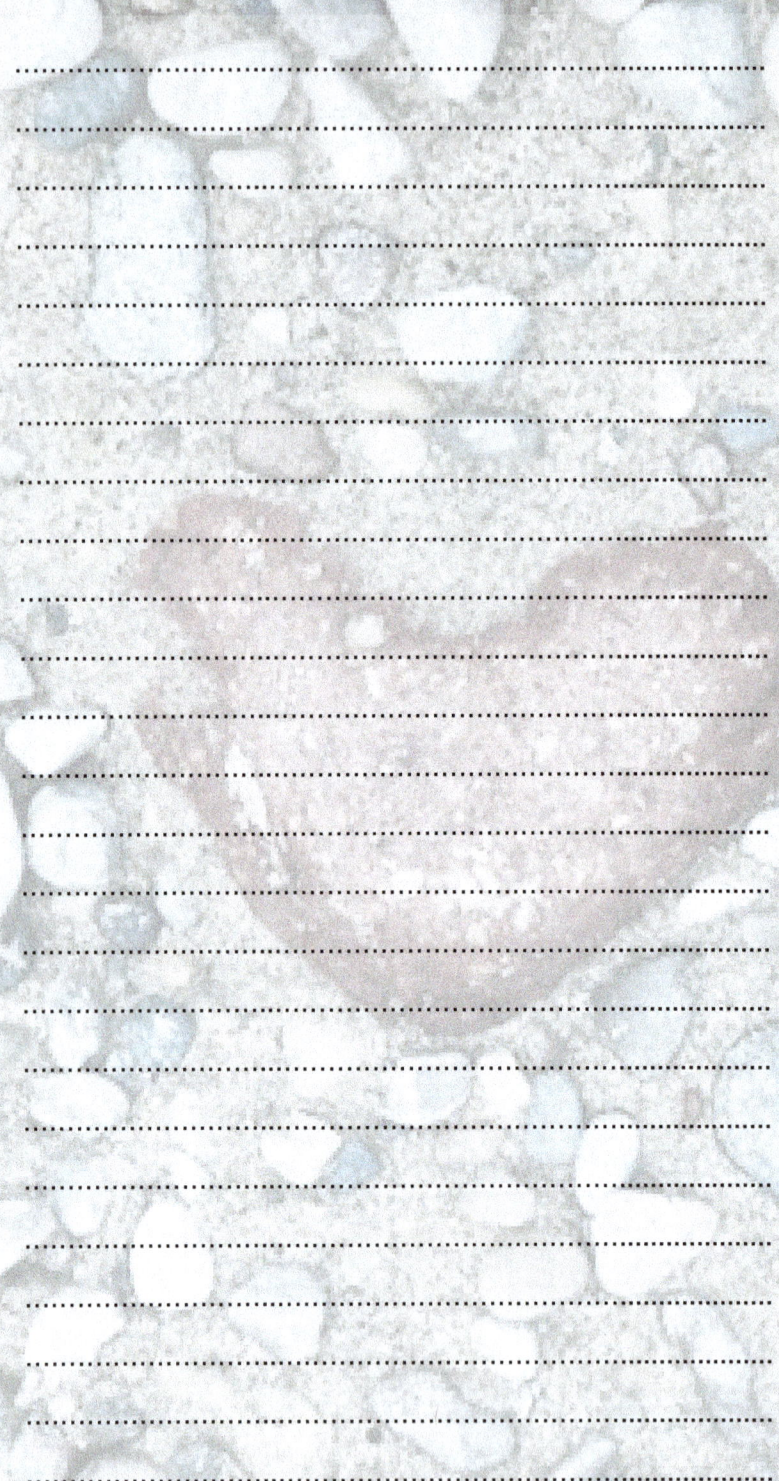

....

....

....

....

....

....

....

....

....

....

....

....

....

....

....

....

....

....

....

....

....

....

....

"For God so loved the world, that He gave His only begotten Son, that whoever believes in Him shall not perish, but have eternal life. For God did not send the Son into the world to judge the world, but that the world might be saved through Him." John 3:16-17 (NASB)

....
....
....
....
....
....
....
....
....
....
....
....
....
....
....
....
....
....
....
....
....
....
....

"I give you a new command: Love one another. Just as I have loved you, you must also love one another." John 13:34 (HCSB)

....
....
....
....
....
....
....
....
....
....
....
....
....
....
....
....
....
....
....
....
....
....

*"Before the mountains were born, and before you created
the earth and the world, you are God. You have always
been, and you will always be." Psalm 90:2 (ICB)*

....

....

....

....

....

....

....

....

....

....

....

....

....

....

....

....

....

....

....

....

*"Your love and kindness are forever; your truth is
as enduring as the heavens." Psalm 89:2 (TLB)*

....

....

....

....

....

....

....

....

....

....

....

....

....

....

....

....

....

"How blessed is God! And what a blessing he is! He's the Father of our Master, Jesus Christ, and takes us to the high places of blessing in him. Long before he laid down earth's foundations, he had us in mind, had settled on us as the focus of his love, to be made whole and holy by his love. Long, long ago he decided to adopt us into his family through Jesus Christ. (What pleasure he took in planning this!) He wanted us to enter into the celebration of his lavish gift-giving by the hand of his beloved Son." Ephesians 1:3-6 (MSG)

....

....

....

....

....

....

....

....

....

....

....

....

....

....

....

....

....

....

....

....

....

....

....

"The Lord is compassionate and gracious, patient, and abundantly rich in gracious love." Psalm 103:8 (ISV)

....

....

....

....

....

....

....

....

....

....

....

....

....

....

....

....

....

"There, I witnessed the glory of the God of Israel storming from the east. His voice thundered like a great waterfall. The entire earth reflected His shining glory." Ezekiel 43:2 (VOICE)

....
....
....
....
....
....
....
....
....
....
....
....
....
....
....
....
....
....
....
....
....

"For You, Lord, are kind and ready to forgive, rich in faithful love to all who call on You." Psalm 86:5 (HCSB)

....
....
....
....
....
....
....
....
....
....
....
....
....
....
....
....
....
....
....
....
....
....
....

"The Lord appeared to him from afar, saying, 'I have loved you with an everlasting love; Therefore I have drawn you with lovingkindness.'" Jeremiah 31:3 (NASB)

....
....
....
....
....
....
....
....
....
....
....
....
....
....
....
....
....
....
....
....
....
....

*"I pray that the Lord will guide you to be as loving as God
and as patient as Christ." 2 Thessalonians 3:5 (CEV)*

....

....

....

....

....

....

....

....

....

....

....

....

....

....

....

....

....

....

....

....

....

....

"When the light shines, it exposes even the dark and shadowy things and turns them into pure reflections of light. This is why they sing, 'Awake, you sleeper! Rise from your grave, and the Anointed One will shine on you.'" Ephesians 5:13-14 (VOICE)

....
....
....
....
....
....
....
....
....
....
....
....
....
....
....
....
....
....
....
....
....
....
....

"May the grace of the Lord Jesus Christ, the love of God, and the fellowship of the Holy Spirit be with you all." 2 Corinthians 13:14 (NLT)

....
....
....
....
....
....
....
....
....
....
....
....
....
....
....
....
....
....
....
....
....
....

"Now may the God who gives endurance and encouragement allow you to live in harmony with one another, according to the command of Christ Jesus ..." Romans 15:5 (HCSB)

....
....
....
....
....
....
....
....
....
....
....
....
....
....
....
....
....
....
....
....
....

"For this very reason do your best to add goodness to your faith; to your goodness add knowledge; to your knowledge add self-control; to your self-control add endurance; to your endurance add godliness; to your godliness add Christian affection; and to your Christian affection add love." 2 Peter 1:5-7 (GNT)

....
....
....
....
....
....
....
....
....
....
....
....
....
....
....
....
....
....
....
....
....

"Therefore, as God's chosen people, holy and dearly loved, clothe yourselves with compassion, kindness, humility, gentleness and patience." Colossians 3:12 (NIV)

Your Free Book is Waiting!

Are you seeking to develop a more intimate Prayer Life with Jesus? Do you want to know what God's Word says about Prayer? Then this beautifully illustrated book is for you!

This "Pray-it-Through" Verse style of Devotional combines a Word Search Puzzle, Sketch Art, and full-size Coloring Pages to create an innovative way *2 Pause and Praise* the Lord. This 72-page offering is a prequel for Deb's other full-size Word Search Puzzle Books. *On Wings of Prayer* will deepen your conversations with the Lord. Here, you'll be encouraged to get into God's Word and sink His precious truths into your heart!

Get your free copy of
On Wings of Prayer here:

Scripture Copyright

Deborah Goshorn-Stenger, and her husband, Douglas

From Deborah's Heart:

Each morning when I rise, I recite Psalm 118:24: *"This is the day that the Lord has made, I will rejoice and be glad in it."* I formed this habit many years ago as a form of praise unto the Lord. It's His gentle reminder that this day is a gift from His hand. This breath is new. These 24 hours hold fresh opportunities to be in His company and get to know Jesus better. It came out of a time of health crisis. In other words—everything in my life was not picturesque or rosy. Yet through these imperfect circumstances, God taught me to praise Him instead of focusing on the difficulty.

This is also where He taught me the beauty and offering of gratitude. Again, for many years, I have practiced thanking God as a method of journaling. I have found that focusing on His goodness, mercy, grace ... whatever He is doing in my life at any given moment ... gives me a documented trail of His blessings and faithfulness. It shows me how He's answering prayers. It helps me discover and unpack truths from His Word. And writing out Scripture is an excellent tool in helping to memorize God's precious promises.

I hope this Verse Journal, with its watercolor-like photo backgrounds that we've taken directly from the Creation's Kaleidoscope, *Embracing Light Devotional*, and the full *Journal*, bring you peace and a deeper communion with Your Abba Daddy. This volume can be taken along with you and makes a great gift. And no matter how you incorporate the ideas for using it, I hope you'll take time to meditate upon each of the Scriptures it contains because each one is God's written communication of His loving nature to your heart.

Blessings,

deborah goshorn-stenger

I hope you've enjoyed Volume I of
Creation's Kaleidoscope: Embracing Light Verse Journal.

Please tell us how this artistically designed open Verse Journal helped you explore your time with the Lord. How did the inscribed verses allow you to pause to notice God's majesty in creation? How did investing your time in journaling, writing prayers, and memorizing Scriptures display God's faithfulness to your heart?

We'd be honored if you left us a review (wherever you've purchased our product). We'll use your feedback to guide any updates to this manuscript and consider your input for future projects.

"Put on your new nature, and be renewed as you learn to know your Creator and become like him. ... Since God chose you to be the holy people he loves, you must clothe yourselves with tenderhearted mercy, kindness, humility, gentleness, and patience. ... Above all, clothe yourselves with love, which binds us all together in perfect harmony. And let the peace that comes from Christ rule in your hearts. For as members of one body you are called to live in peace. And always be thankful. Let the message about Christ, in all its richness, fill your lives. Teach and counsel each other with all the wisdom he gives. Sing psalms and hymns and spiritual songs to God with thankful hearts. And whatever you do or say, do it as a representative of the Lord Jesus, giving thanks through him to God the Father."
Colossians 3:10, 12, & 14-17 (NIV)

Until next time, as always, I wish you
God's richest blessings and joy!

In His Love, *deborah goshorn-stenger*

www.ingramcontent.com/pod-product-compliance
Lightning Source LLC
Chambersburg PA
CBHW061157120626
46546CB00005B/2095